Surprising Things

We Do for
Fun

Saskia Lacey

Consultants

Timothy Rasinski, Ph.D.
Kent State University

Lori Oczkus, M.A.
Literacy Consultant

Publishing Credits

Rachelle Cracchiolo, M.S.Ed., *Publisher*
Conni Medina, M.A.Ed., *Managing Editor*
Dona Herweck Rice, *Series Developer*
Emily R. Smith, M.A.Ed., *Content Director*
Stephanie Bernard/Noelle Cristea, M.A.Ed., *Editors*
Robin Erickson, *Senior Graphic Designer*

Image Credits: Cover and p.1 age fotostock/Alamy Stock Photo; p.4 Jeff
J Mitchell/Getty Images; p.6 Target Presse Agentur Gmbh/Getty Images;
pp.6–7 Philip Scalia/Alamy Stock Photo; p.7 Darryl Torckler/Getty Images;
p.8 Jaap Arriens/Alamy Stock Photo; p.9 Jaap Arriens/NurPhoto/NurPhoto
via Getty Images; pp.10–11 david pearson/Alamy Stock Photo; pp.12–13
Charles McQuillan/Getty Images; p.17 Slaven Vlasic/Getty Images; p.20 Paul
Fleet/Alamy Stock Photo; pp.26–27 Photo by Brett Erickson; p.29 ZUMA
Press, Inc./Alamy Stock Photo; pp.38–39 Stephen Chung/Alamy Live News;
p.40 Al Freni/The LIFE Images Collection/Getty Images; p.42 Bobby Bank/
WireImage/Getty Images; p.44 Adam Taylor/ABC via Getty Images; p.45
Everett Collection Historical/Alamy Stock Photo; p.48 Fernando Leon/Getty
Images; p.52 David Peevers/Getty Images; p.57 WENN Ltd/Alamy Stock
Photo; p.61 age fotostock/Alamy Stock Photo; all other images from iStock
and/or Shutterstock.

Teacher Created Materials
5301 Oceanus Drive
Huntington Beach, CA 92649-1030
http://www.tcmpub.com
ISBN 978-1-4938-3638-3
© 2017 Teacher Created Materials, Inc.

Table of Contents

Welcome to Planet Weird

There's simply no excuse for boredom in today's world. Modern life is chock-full of the brilliantly bizarre and the too-strange-to-be-true. If you find yourself complaining that there's nothing to do on weekends, you're not looking hard enough! So take notes, choose a hobby, and make it a surprising one.

The various activities in this book may be strange, out of the ordinary, or just plain interesting. In this book, you'll learn about the most peculiar **pastimes** on the planet. Ever heard of the Mud Olympics (mud soccer, anyone?) or outhouse racing (yes, you read that right)? Some of these activities might sound a little *too* weird, but keep an open mind. You might discover your life's true calling as an underwater hockey player or bog snorkeler. Well, maybe not, but anything's possible— even the truly surprising and bizarre!

Once Strange, Now Popular!

Some of our most beloved hobbies were once considered super strange. Though it's been around since at least the seventeenth century, surfing only became part of popular culture in the 1950s.

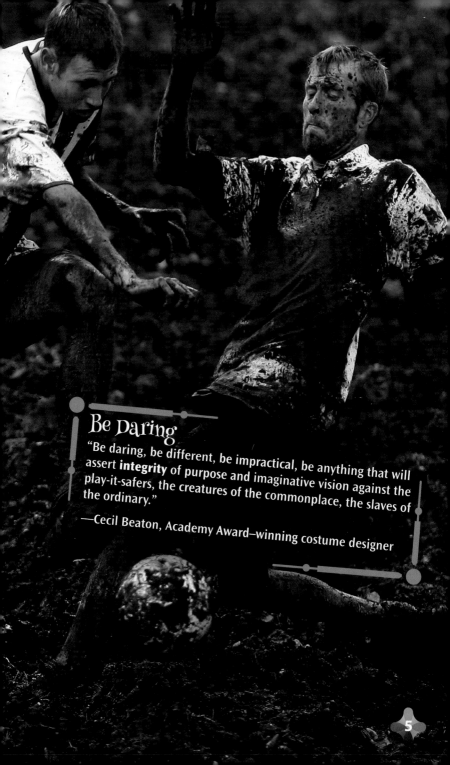

Be Daring

"Be daring, be different, be impractical, be anything that will assert **integrity** of purpose and imaginative vision against the play-it-safers, the creatures of the commonplace, the slaves of the ordinary."

—Cecil Beaton, Academy Award–winning costume designer

Absurd Athletics

Whether you prefer your sports on land or water, somewhere in the world is just the mash-up activity for you! For the intense physical and intellectual competitor, chessboxing is a tailor-made sport. Those interested in pure, free-spirited fun might find pumpkin kayaking to be the perfect pastime.

Chessboxing

The origin of chessboxing is questionable. Some people say a graphic novel, *Cold Equator*, inspired the sport. Others think the idea of chessboxing originated in the 1979 kung fu movie, *Mystery of Chessboxing*. Either way, the game is now popular all over the world, from Los Angeles to Berlin.

In this grueling sport, athletes must use both brains and brawn during alternating rounds of chess and boxing. Rounds usually last between two and four minutes. Competitors can win either by checkmate or knockout.

Unicycle Football

Since taking a dive on concrete is far more dangerous than on a grassy field, tackling in unicycle football is not as aggressive. In this game, players wear flags, and a "tackle" means removing them from another player or gently knocking the opponent off his or her unicycle.

Octopush

Octopush is underwater hockey. Players wear snorkels and fins, and use a glove with a small stick to push around the puck.

Giant Pumpkin Kayaking

This mash-up is pure, silly fun. Participants board gigantic, hollowed-out pumpkins and race across Tualatin Lake in Oregon.

Bossaball

Bossaball combines gymnastics, volleyball, soccer, and an inflatable court. Sound fun? Developed by Filip Eyckmans between 2003 and 2005, the sport is now played all over the world. Bossaball tournaments take place in France, Saudi Arabia, Ecuador, Romania, Turkey, the Netherlands, and the Czech Republic.

Music plays a big role in bossaball, making every game feel like a performance. Samba referees oversee the games and entertain the audiences, acting as MCs, DJs, or drummers.

Inspired by a style of music called *bossa nova*, bossaball incorporates style and attitude. Each game is energized by music and rhythm. Players use the Brazilian martial art, **capoeira**, to infuse their gameplay with **rhythmic** acrobatics.

STOP! THINK...

- What kind of skills or abilities does a person need to succeed at bossaball?
- Why do you think there is a point range for scoring?
- How do you think Eyckmans decided on the scoring rubric?

Bossaball by the Numbers

- **25 points**—Teams score 1 point when the ball lands on the gray part of the inflatable court, 3 points when it lands on the trampoline, and 5 points for not using their hands. You need 25 points to win!

- **8–10 players total**—Each team is made up of 4 to 5 players.

- **3–5 sets**—The team that wins the best of 5 is the winner!

- **2 goalkeepers**—Each team has a goalkeeper who tries to keep the other team from scoring on the trampoline.

- **2 trampolines**—There is a trampoline on each side of the net. Players use it for acrobatic attacks.

- **1 inflatable court with a net**—The bossaball court ranges in size and includes a net similar to a volleyball net.

Worm Charming

People are always on the hunt for new absurd activities, but worm charming may take the cake. Every year, in the English town of Willaston, people flock to participate in the World Worm Charming Championship (WWCC).

Worm charming is a method of raising worms from the ground through the use of vibration. The activity has been around since 1980, when Tom Shufflebotham charmed more than 500 worms in half an hour. Since then, a set of rules and **regulations** for worm charming has been devised. Each person is given a 9.8 by 9.8 foot (3 by 3 meter) plot. Music can be used to entice the worms from underground, but digging is strictly forbidden. Competitors usually use garden forks to help the process. The garden fork is stuck into the ground and jiggled to create vibrations. The competitor who has charmed the most worms by the end of the 30 minutes is awarded a trophy from the WWCC. The trophy itself features a golden wiggling worm!

The Gillie

If you're too squeamish to pick up the worms you've charmed, you may appoint a second charmer to complete the task. This person is known as a *Gillie*.

Unusual Equipment

A four-tined garden fork is the most popular worm-charming tool. Competitors have found that the most successful way to charm a worm is to stick the fork about 6 inches (15 centimeters) into the ground and vibrate the tool by hand.

Extreme Ironing

Though it's been around for a while, extreme ironing is a sport that continues to surprise people. **Enthusiasts** of the unusual activity are continually finding new ways to iron. Extreme ironers are known to practice their pastime in remote and dangerous locations. In the past, the sport has been practiced while bicycling, mountain climbing, swimming, water-skiing, and even skydiving! The future of this wild and diverse sport is truly limitless, often combining multiple sports at a time. It is as much extreme sport as it is performance art.

Outhouse Racing

Outhouse racing teams are similar to car racing pit crews. One person "drives" the outhouse while other teammates push, pull, and tug the port-a-potty across the track.

Bog Snorkeling

Ready, set, gross! Bog snorkeling, which has been around since the mid-1970s, was first played in Wales in the United Kingdom. Competitors wear snorkeling gear and race their way through as many as 145 yards (133 meters) of the muck in a **peat bog**. The catch? Participants cannot use standard swimming strokes—they have to power through using just their feet!

A Guide to Muggle Quidditch

Brooms up! It's time to play muggle quidditch. J. K. Rowling invented quidditch within the Harry Potter universe. In the books, teams of wizards and witches battle sky-high on broomsticks. Unfortunately in real-life muggle quidditch, there's no flying.

The Players

Each team has seven players:

- ◎ **1 seeker**—The seeker's job is to hunt for the snitch.
- ◎ **1 keeper**—Keepers defend the goal hoops.
- ◎ **2 beaters**—Beaters try to peg the opposing team with bludgers.
- ◎ **3 chasers**—Chasers score points for their team by throwing the quaffle through the goal hoops.

The Field

A quidditch field is called the *pitch*. It is usually an oval that is 48 yards (43.9 meters) long. The field is divided in half, with three goal hoops and a keeper's zone on each side. Players run around the field, avoiding the bludgers, attempting to score goals using the quaffle, and trying to catch the golden snitch.

The Equipment and Rules

Quaffle—When chasers throw the quaffle (often a volleyball) through the goal hoops, their team is awarded 10 points.

Bludgers—When team members are hit with one of the three bludgers (usually dodgeballs), they must drop any balls they are holding, return to their goal hoops, and touch the goal hoop before returning to the game.

Golden Snitch—Unlike in the Harry Potter series, the snitch is not a small object but rather a person. When the seeker finds the snitch, his or her team is awarded 30 points and the game is over.

Trading Lives

For some of us, playing pretend never gets old. When we were young, we had all the time in the world to build forts and imagine worlds of princesses and pirates. Now, between balancing academics and extracurriculars, finding time is tricky. But don't fret, fellow pretenders, there are plenty of adults out there who've figured out a way to get their fix of imaginary fun.

Comic-Con

The San Diego Comic-Con hosts well over 100,000 fans, volunteers, and special guests of all ages. Costumes and role-playing are encouraged and celebrated. The four-day event is so popular that tickets sell out lightning fast. Fans are eager to spend time with fellow admirers and get dressed up as their favorite characters from comic books, movies, and TV shows. Some fans sit in on their favorite DC Comics™ and Marvel® **panels** or visit the booths of their favorite characters.

The Masquerade Ball

Every year, the San Diego Comic-Con hosts various costume contests. In 2015, a cable channel sponsored a **masquerade** ball where contestants **vied** for awards including Best Original Design, Best Workmanship, Most Humorous, and Best Young Fan.

Anime Expo®

The Los Angeles Anime Expo celebrates all things anime. **Cosplayers** compete in competitions, meet up with others in their fandoms, and take pictures in professionally built sets.

Virtual Reality at Long Last?

One of the simplest and quickest ways to "trade lives" is through role-playing video games. Each game presents a different quest or adventure, one that instantly transports you into the world of your **avatar**. But is there a way to make the gaming experience even more **immersive**?

Gamers have been experimenting with virtual reality (VR) for a long time. Again and again, the idea of a new form of gaming has been teased, but the results have been largely disappointing. But there is hope! High-powered VR is becoming, well, a reality.

Virtual Universes

The options, challenges, and number of planets in *No Man's Sky* make it practically infinite. The major selling point? It is procedurally generated. Each planet that a player navigates to is created as he or she plays.

Speedrunning and Sequence Breaking

Speedrunners try to finish their games as quickly as possible. These impressive players "speed" through complex games in mere hours when the games take most people weeks to conquer. Sequence breakers know video games inside and out. They use flaws in the games' designs to their advantages, developing tricks to skip obstacles and rack up points.

In 2016, the first VR devices for consumers were released. Among the most anticipated were the Oculus Rift, Facebook's VR headset, Sony's VR Playstation, and HTC's Vive. Reviews were mixed. Gamers **bemoaned** the costs of the headsets, which required software and cost over $1,000 each. But, many users were impressed with VR that included motion tracking, allowing gamers to move through games without the distraction of game controllers.

Steampunk: Just Add Water

Imagine you're on a modern tablet and notice it has three percent power left. But you don't reach for the charger—you reach for a glass of water! The tablet can recharge itself with steam. This is just a part of steampunk. It's the literary genre that has spilled over into fashion, technology, and even lifestyles!

Steampunk has no hard and fast rules. But there are a few basic guidelines that most people will agree steampunk adheres to: the technology should be modern, objects need to be powered by something other than electricity, and the setting is generally the English Victorian era of the 1800s. Picture a vintage typewriter with a high-tech screen or a flying boat powered by coal, and you get the idea. Steampunk has also branched into fashion, and people have created unique looks based on it.

What's with the "Punk"?

While the *steam* in steampunk is obvious, the *punk* refers to the idea of going against convention and being your own person.

Read All About It!

Interested in reading steampunk books? Check out the Leviathan series by author Scott Westerfeld about teenagers Alek and Deryn in an alternate early twentieth century Europe.

Welcome to fantasy football! Sports enthusiasts can find all the glory, all the action . . . and none of the injuries. The concept is simple enough: friends, family, or **acquaintances** form a league and act as the managers and coaches for their own teams. They draft real football players and earn points based on what these players do in the actual games. For example, a fantasy team might earn one point per ten yards receiving and six points for a touchdown that is made during an actual game played by the professionals.

In some leagues, these points add up over the course of the season, and the person with the most points at the end of it wins. In smaller leagues, the matchups are tracked week to week, and teams hope to make the playoffs based off their weekly scores. Winners get bragging rights and maybe cash prizes. With an estimated 57 million players in 2016, this fantasy has become a multibillion-dollar reality.

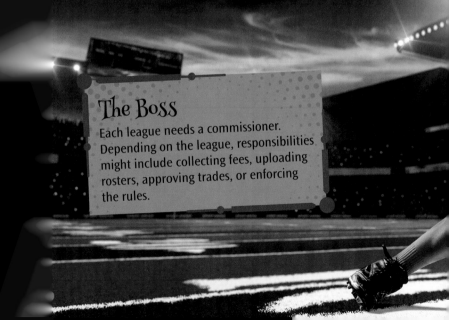

The Boss

Each league needs a commissioner. Depending on the league, responsibilities might include collecting fees, uploading rosters, approving trades, or enforcing the rules.

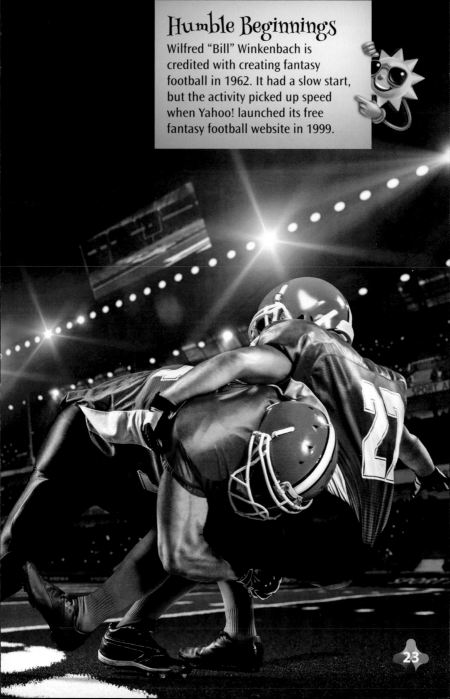

Humble Beginnings

Wilfred "Bill" Winkenbach is credited with creating fantasy football in 1962. It had a slow start, but the activity picked up speed when Yahoo! launched its free fantasy football website in 1999.

It sounds wild, but it's undeniable, and some people may consider it unfortunate. The world is full of people a tad obsessed with their pets.

An Unfortunately True Story

Unfortunate fact: there are people who will halt traffic to meet, hug, and converse with your dog. It's weird and tolerably annoying, and likely they can't help themselves—such is the plight of those **infatuated with animals!**

You can find pet fanatics everywhere; people share cute animal photos over social media and even create separate profiles for their cats, dogs, pigs, and reptiles. You probably know someone who is totally obsessed with his or her pet. Or maybe *you* are that someone. This chapter is a salute to pet fanatics who take animal appreciation to the next level.

The Pig Olympics

Russia hosts a playful annual tournament known as the Pig Olympics. The animals run short races, swim, and play "pigball."

Almost Twins

Can it be? A pet and owner look-alike contest? This is pet passion at its finest. Thank you Bloomington, Minnesota, for hosting the "Most Twinning Pet and Owner" competition.

To Be a Pet Parent

Meet Lily, a Cavalier King Charles spaniel and cocker spaniel mix. She's eight years old (56 in dog years) and is pretty much the world's sweetest creature. Talking about Lily comes easily for me, as it does for many pet owners. Angling the conversation back to her unique wonderfulness and latest achievements in cuteness happens quite often.

When it comes to pet pride, there is always another way to become even more ridiculously obsessed with your furry friend. From taking countless photos on cell phones, to carrying your lovable pet around in a purse, to arranging play dates for your pet, it's easier than ever to become entirely obsessed. There are even pet strollers, pet camps, and pet condos.

Mindful Petitations™

For those who love **meditating** and spending time with their pets, petitation is the hobby of choice. This pet-centered activity encourages people to connect with their pets through mindful meditation.

Pug Love

St. Louis hosts a meet-up group that is pug specific. Pug owners gather to celebrate the stout and wrinkly breed and let their dogs socialize with each other.

Pet-tastic Getaways

Some people may believe that the only place for pets is at home. But for those of us who are pet obsessed, we like to pamper our furry friends with special animal getaways.

Condos for Kittens

Looking for a condo for your kitty? Have no fear, Morris Animal Inn in Morristown, New Jersey, is here. The inn's accommodations range from two-level, single-occupancy condos to luxury suites, where cats can live the fine feline life in a swanky, multi-level paradise. Boarding areas come complete with miniature furniture and places to climb, nap, and play.

The Morris Animal Inn also promises to keep your kitty entertained with "quiet lap and brushing time," "story time," and "views of beautiful fish tanks." Cats can feast on gourmet prepared treats from the sea. They can even be taken on "walks" in the Kitty SUV, a covered vehicle that allows cats to explore the outdoors without running away.

Camp Dogwood

Camp Dogwood, located in Rimforest, California, is just one of many summer camps made for both dog owners and their canine companions. Human campers can do crafts, such as build dog beds, or attend lectures about how to keep their pets entertained during the cold winter months. There are fun ways to test a dog's "discgility" with challenging flying disc games. There are even dog massage classes. Owners can treat their furry friends to relaxing, calming massages before playtime.

Adventure Unleashed

This company offers canine classes such as dog parkour, which teach dogs how to engage with their surroundings in active and fun ways. According to the company, dog parkour helps increase "balance, coordination, strength, and focus."

Essentials for Animal Enthusiasts

One easy way to spot a fellow pet-lover is to count the number of animal or pet accessories they own. People who adore animals can't help buying toys, clothes, and other presents for their pets.

Obstacle Course—Create an indoor playground to keep your pet entertained during cold winter months.

Pet Jewelry—Don't be afraid to deck your pet out with extra **glitz**. Just make sure your animal is comfortable wearing the new bling!

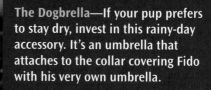

The Dogbrella—If your pup prefers to stay dry, invest in this rainy-day accessory. It's an umbrella that attaches to the collar covering Fido with his very own umbrella.

Bacon Bubble Blower—Bubbles + bacon = best canine gift ever!

The Goldfish Walker—Just because your pet is a fish, doesn't mean that you can't spend some quality time together outdoors. The goldfish walker is proof! It's an aquarium on wheels!

Dog Snuggie®—Get a Snuggie for your favorite cuddle buddy and help him or her stay warm! Just like a person, your pooch can also wear a blanket.

Pet Strollers—Want to pretend your fur baby is the real deal? Increase the weirdness of your pet mania by pushing your little fuzz ball around in a stroller.

Don't Try This at Home!

Be sure to consult a professional if you even *think* about trying any of the activities mentioned in this chapter!

Slacklining

Slacklining is one part tightrope walking and two parts acrobatics. The degree of danger depends on the slackliner's level of experience. Beginners tie their lines close to the ground so they won't be injured if they fall. More advanced slackliners tie their lines high above the ground and attempt more challenging tricks.

Over time, even more dangerous variations of slacklining have developed. These variations include highlining, which is slacklining at great heights, and waterlining, which is slacklining over water.

Tricklining

Tricklining is the combination of the seriously extraordinary with the seriously dangerous. A **variant** of slacklining, tricklining consists of dangerous stunts done while balancing on a line. Some of the most advanced tricks include front flips and back flips.

Yogalining

A low lunge may be easy on the ground, but imagine trying the pose 50 feet (15.2 meters) in the air on a tightrope! Yogalining combines yoga poses and slacklining.

Wingsuiting is one of the most dangerous hobby choices. It takes a truly fearless person to attempt this sport. Resembling gigantic flying squirrels, wingsuiters float, spin, and dive through the air.

One of the first wingsuiting attempts happened over a hundred years ago in Paris, France. In 1912, a tailor named Franz Reichelt jumped off the Eiffel Tower wearing a handmade wingsuit. Reichelt's suit was ineffective; the jump was fatal.

In the following decades, other adventurists would make similar attempts. Some were successful, while others were not. It was not until the 1990s that semi-reliable wingsuits were developed. The sport soon became popular within the skydiving community.

Today, wingsuiters are always trying to push the limits. They set new records every year as they dive from aircrafts and go **BASE jumping** from high peaks. In 2013, Valery Rozov set one of the most impressive wingsuiting records, jumping from the north side of Mount Everest—some 23,680 feet (7,220 meters) in the air.

Wingboarding

Wingboarding is often compared to wakeboarding. As with wakeboarding, the rider is towed at high speeds. So, what's the major difference? Wingboarders surf clouds, not waves, and they are towed by planes instead of boats.

Poweriser Stilts

Weird? Yep. Dangerous? Definitely. Poweriser stilts are sort of like high-tech pogo sticks. People run, jump, flip, and attempt tricky stunts while wearing them.

Outrageous Obstacle Courses

Inspired by the popular television show *American Ninja Warrior*, obstacle courses continue to become stranger and more dangerous. One of the most brutal of the bunch is a British race known as the Tough Guy®. Those who are brave enough to face the Tough Guy challenge could have to crawl under razor wire, swim through freezing water, cross fire pits, climb 50-foot (15-meter) towers, and crawl through underground tunnels. The race is usually 9 miles (15 kilometers) in length and has resulted in two **fatalities**. Can you say "seriously dangerous"?

Antarctic 100k®

If you want to participate in the Antarctic 100k, you better be able to run 62 miles (100 kilometers). Sound doable? Now, add freezing weather with temperatures around −13°F (−25°C) and ice cold winds. As if that's not enough, this race takes place on a glacier!

Spartan's Death Race®

The tagline of the Death Race is "You May Die"—they're not sugarcoating it. If you're interested, the company provides opportunities worldwide to partake. However, the race limits the number of competitors, and the obstacles, events, and start time are kept a secret until the day of the event to test participant flexibility. Past challenges have involved doing physically demanding work that benefits the local community, such as bridge building. There are also grueling mental tasks, such as perfecting the craft of folding origami cranes. These intense races can last several days!

World's Toughest Mudder

This event occurs in locations all around the globe. It's is a 5-mile (8-kilometer) course and includes military-style obstacles. Competitors must loop through the course for 24 hours straight. Sound impossible? It nearly is.

THINK LINK

- What do you think is the appeal of participating in dangerous races or obstacle courses?

- What are some of the potential dangers of running a marathon in below-freezing conditions?

Dangerous Foods

Do you love seriously spicy food? You can call yourself a pyro-gourmaniac. If your taste buds are up to the challenge, there is a world of spicy eating contests waiting for you. Take the chile-eating contest in Hatch, New Mexico, for example. There, competitors fight to eat the greatest number of chiles. It's a good idea to be an avid lover of chiles if you enter this competition—the highest prize is a 40-pound (18-kilogram) bag of chiles—in case the winner didn't get his or her fill!

The Curry Contest

In Edinburgh, Scotland, there is a spicy food challenge so legendary that the British Red Cross has to stand by in case one of the contestants needs medical care. The most dangerous dish is called the Kismot Killer Curry, a fiery mix that includes five of the world's hottest chiles.

Atomic Chicken Wings

Before contestants can participate in Quaker Steak & Lube's Atomic Hot Wing Challenge, they must sign a medical waiver. In the past, patrons of the restaurant have fainted after eating the legendarily spicy wings.

The Ghost Pepper

At the Clifton Chilli Club's Chilli-Eating Contest, spicy-food lovers take turns eating incredibly hot chile peppers, including the spiciest chile on Earth, the ghost pepper. This chile pepper can be anywhere from 2 to 10 times hotter than the average habanero.

Then and Now

The concept of what's fun has changed a lot through the decades! Check out these blast-from-the-past ways to enjoy life, and their contemporary counterparts.

Adopt-A-Pet

Pets are adorable and lovable, but they can be expensive and time-consuming, too. Luckily, Gary Dahl had a simple (and **lucrative**!) solution. In 1975 he rolled out the perfect pet—the Pet Rock. Dahl bought beach stones for a penny each and packaged them in cardboard carrying cases with air holes. There was even a "Pet Rock Training Manual" so proud owners could train their rocks to sit, attack, and play dead. It might sound ridiculous, but consumers didn't think so—they purchased 1.5 million Pet Rocks.

It Cost How Much?

Pet Rocks sold for $3.95 in 1975. That would be equivalent to $18.00 in 2016!

IMPORTANT: Open box carefully. DO NOT remove rock before reading instructions.

This box contains one genuine pedigreed

PET ROCK

Today, people prefer their "pets" to be a little more technologically advanced. A quick Internet search will return numerous robot pets available on the market. As coding becomes more straightforward, the number of items that allow people not just to use technology but also to interact with it is on the rise. For anyone interested in constructing and programming their own pet robots, the Ohbot is a dream come true. It has even begun making its way into schools in the United Kingdom.

artificial intelligence robots

A New Breed

The Ohbot can be purchased preassembled for a bit more than the unassembled version. There is even a sound effects pack that can be purchased separately that includes 3,000 everyday sounds to truly bring the Ohbot to life!

Challenge Accepted!

According to folklore, four immigrants held a hot-dog-eating contest to prove their patriotism. The event occurred on July 4, 1916, at Nathan's Famous®, a hot dog stand in Brooklyn, New York. The contest continues each year; but now it has rules, qualifying rounds, and wildcard spots—plus a $10,000 prize.

Other eating competitions were popular in the past, too. Pie-eating contests at carnivals and fairs challenged contestants to eat the fastest. Participants' hands were often tied behind their backs, ensuring some good, messy fun.

Changing Times

Jim Mullen was the unofficial first winner of Nathan's challenge. In 1916, he ate 13 hot dogs. The 2016 winner, Joey Chestnut, shown below, ate 70!

A completely different challenge swept the world via social media in 2014. Millions of people were nominated to participate in the ALS Ice Bucket Challenge. The goal was to fight a neurological disease called ALS, which stands for amyotrophic lateral sclerosis. The people who were nominated had two choices: do the challenge or make a donation to the ALS Association. Those who accepted the challenge posted videos of buckets or coolers of icy water being dumped on their heads. In all, the challenge raised more than $100 million. The millions of wet, shivering donors helped bring awareness about this disease simply by posting their videos.

Waste Not, Want Not

Actor Matt Damon used clean toilet water for his ice bucket challenge to bring attention to the lack of clean water around the world.

Smooth Moves

Clean-cut teenagers in Philadelphia rushed to the studio, hoping to be first in line to audition. Millions of other teens across the country rushed home from school to turn on their TVs. It was all for *American Bandstand*, a show that played Top 40 music and filmed ordinary teenagers dancing.

Teen viewers learned the latest dance moves and the most popular songs. But they also heard reviews about new music and kept tabs on their favorite dancers. The show aired from 1952 to 1989, covering many genres of music.

Similarly, in the summer of 2005, ABC quietly filled an open slot with a new show. Executives wondered if mixing celebrities with dancing would be a winning combination. *Dancing with the Stars* exploded with a popularity no one could have predicted! Pairing a celebrity with a professional dancer, the show has couples perform choreographed routines each week. Their scores are based on a panel of judges and votes from the at-home audience. The couple with the lowest score is eliminated the following week. The last couple dancing is declared the winner and awarded the coveted disco ball trophy.

From Across the Pond

Dancing with the Stars is based on the British show *Strictly Come Dancing*.

"It's Got a Good Beat and You Can Dance to It!"

This review was given about so many songs, by so many dancers, it has become synonymous with *American Bandstand*.

From interactive television shows to apps combining real-life with the digital world, many people expect more from their entertainment than to simply sit and watch. Check out ways audience members can become participants.

Pokémon GO®

Heads are down, phones are out, and people wander sidewalks and parks as though looking for something. It may seem strange to an outsider, but insiders know what's going on—Pokémon GO! The app was introduced in the summer of 2016 and had millions of users within a few short weeks.

The game uses augmented reality to merge the cyber world and real world together. When players or "trainers" have the app open on their phones, the animated Pokémon® creatures appear on their screens superimposed over reality. The goal is to catch, train, and battle. Using the app's map, trainers are on the lookout for shaking bushes (a Pokémon is near!), PokéStops (find needed items like potions and Poké Balls), and Gyms (places to battle other trainers in heavily populated areas). It might be a short-lived craze, but it gets players out of their houses, seeing new places, and meeting new people!

What's in a Name?

The name Pokémon comes from a combination of the words *pocket* and *monster*.

Old School

The original Pokémon game came out in 1996 for the Nintendo Game Boy®. A player's goal is to become a master by catching, training, and trading all 151 Pokémon.

Reality TV

Reality TV is everywhere in prime time these days. The show credited with being the first reality show actually aired on a music channel! MTV premiered *The Real World®* in 1992. With a different cast and new location for each season, it follows the lives of seven 18- to 25-year-old strangers living together. Eight years after *The Real World* debuted, a major network took a chance on *Survivor®*, a new type of reality show. Contestants are left in a deserted location with no food or shelter. They vote each other off the island one by one, and the last contestant remaining receives a $1,000,000 prize.

America was hooked, and dozens of reality TV shows flooded the airwaves. Many shows are competitions, such as *Survivor* and *Chopped*. *Shark Tank®* gives hopeful **entrepreneurs** the chance to turn their ideas into businesses by convincing panel members to invest their money. *American Idol* let the audience choose which singers stay and which go home. Other shows simply follow the lives of the participants, giving viewers a glimpse into someone else's oftentimes crazy life.

Rags to Riches

Some reality alumni became big-time celebrities. Academy Award® winning actress Jennifer Hudson and Grammy Award® winning singer Carrie Underwood were both on *American Idol*.

Too Much of a Good Thing?

More than 300 reality TV shows have been broadcast! Did anyone catch *Amish in the City* or *I Wanna Marry "Harry"*? Both shows flopped fast.

OUTWIT OUTPLAY

SURVIVOR

PALAU

OUTLAST

Finding Like Minds

Whether you live in a small town or a big city, it can be a challenge to find others who partake in your favorite hobbies. If you find yourself alone in your obsession with Pig Latin poetry, or if you want to bond with other dungeon game fanatics, worry not. There's a land of infinite connections where you're sure to find like minds—the Internet. If used safely, the Internet can help anyone find people who engage in similar hobbies.

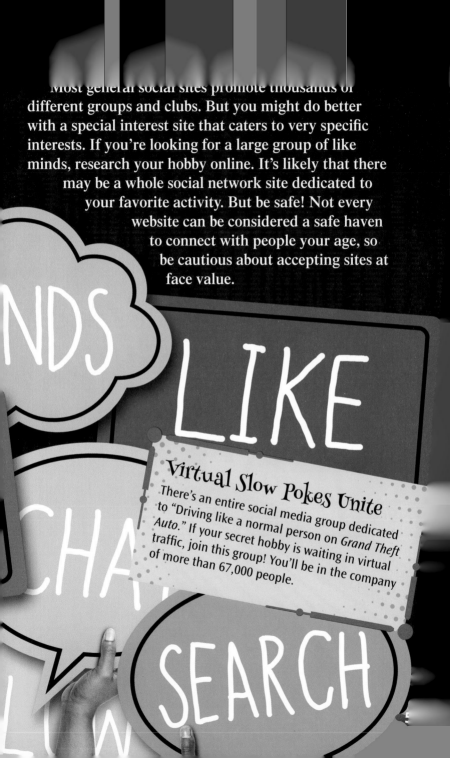

Most general social sites promote thousands of different groups and clubs. But you might do better with a special interest site that caters to very specific interests. If you're looking for a large group of like minds, research your hobby online. It's likely that there may be a whole social network site dedicated to your favorite activity. But be safe! Not every website can be considered a safe haven to connect with people your age, so be cautious about accepting sites at face value.

Virtual Slow Pokes Unite

There's an entire social media group dedicated to "Driving like a normal person on *Grand Theft Auto*." If your secret hobby is waiting in virtual traffic, join this group! You'll be in the company of more than 67,000 people.

Chills and Thrills

Seeking a social circle of people who love watching and creating scary movies? Seattle's Horror Filmmakers Club invites fellow "dreadfuls" to network and collaborate. Similar groups can be found throughout the United States.

Freeze Frame

If unusual art is your thing, you're sure to find others with similar interests at the Pageant of the Masters. The festival, held in Laguna Beach, California, is described as a "90-minute stage show of 'living pictures.'" The pageant features art re-creations of classical and contemporary paintings and sculptures. In other words, real people are made to look like figures from works of art.

The Pageant of the Masters stages great works such as Leonardo da Vinci's *The Last Supper*. The festival has featured paintings by Paul Cezanne, Henri Matisse, and Frida Kahlo. Each work of live art poses for 90 seconds. The people in the paintings or sculptures try their best to stay as still as possible. Hundreds of volunteers help the paintings come to life. The event is so popular that volunteers have to be turned away. Each year, over a 100,000 people attend the festival!

Constructing Shadows

You step into a gallery and see a strange pile of objects on the floor. The objects appear to be random, but when you take a closer look, you notice that they are casting beautiful shadows. You've stumbled upon shadow art! If you find this concept intriguing, consider finding an art show that highlights this unique art form.

Anti-Socializers

There might be plenty of reasons why you want to avoid hanging out with others. Maybe you're too lazy to leave the couch, or maybe you, like many **introverts**, just prefer the peace and quiet of your own **abode**. Truthfully, you don't need a single reason for why you'd rather be alone than in a big group. But whatever your reason, there are groups that cater to your unique needs, such as the Atlanta-based group called the Anti-socialites or the Nevada Camping for Lazy People group, which enjoys camping—as long as there's no physical activity required.

Shh!

If silence is your favorite sound, there are many groups that celebrate the absence of noise. Take the Silent Reading Party in New York City, where people gather to read quietly in the same space. There are also silent film enthusiasts and silent hiking clubs.

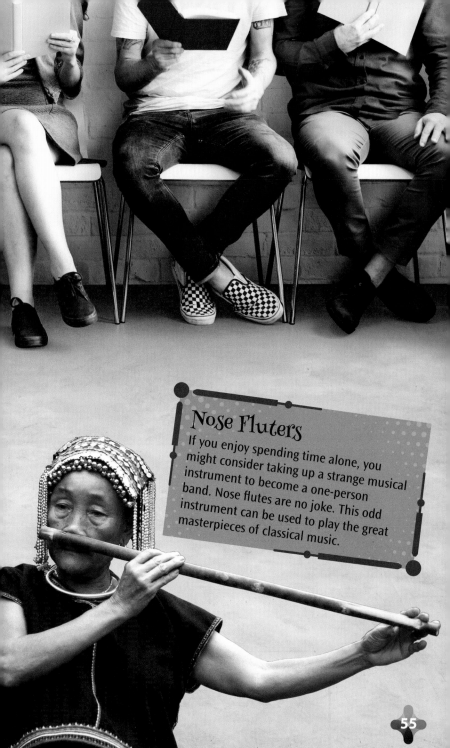

Nose Fluters

If you enjoy spending time alone, you might consider taking up a strange musical instrument to become a one-person band. Nose flutes are no joke. This odd instrument can be used to play the great masterpieces of classical music.

Looking to the Future

We live in strange times, indeed. There are fascinating sports like bog snorkeling, bossaball, and muggle quidditch. There are dangerous hobbies that range from tricklining to hot chili pepper-eating contests. Some people take part in unusual obsessions with comic books, pet competitions, or masquerade balls.

Still, while there are many surprising hobbies in the world, there are plenty left to be discovered—or invented! If odd sports like octopush and chessboxing aren't your thing and dangerous activities such as wingsuiting or the Death Race sound too frightening, maybe what you're looking for hasn't been created. It might be time to put on your inventor's cap! The world could be much better (and stranger!) for it.

Lazy Soccer

So you want to play soccer but can't be bothered to stand up? Lazy soccer can be played from two chairs with attachable nets.

Ping-Pong Door

Perfect for small spaces, this ingenious invention is exactly what it sounds like: a door that doubles as a ping-pong table.

Glossary

abode—home or residence

acquaintances—people you may know but are not close to

avatar—small image or graphic that represents a player or user

BASE jumping—parachute jumping off a building, an antenna, a structure or Earth

bemoaned—complained about

capoeira—a Brazilian martial art that is based around dancelike movement

cosplayers—people who dress up as characters from movies, books, or video games

enthusiasts—people who enjoy something very much

entrepreneurs—people willing to start businesses even if they might lose money before they make any

fatalities—deaths resulting from disaster

glitz—flashiness

immersive—deeply involving one's senses to possibly create an altered mental state

infatuated—inspired by a passion for

integrity—the quality of being moral and honest

introverts—people who need to spend time alone but may also enjoy spending time with others

lucrative—creating profit or wealth

masquerade—a party or gathering where people wear masks and other disguises

meditating—spending time in silence; clearing the mind

panels—groups of people who discuss and answer questions in front of an audience

pastimes—hobbies

peat bog—a wet, muddy body of water that has accumulated dead plant materials

regulations—laws or rules that are enforced by an authority

rhythmic—having a regular repeated pattern of sounds or movements

variant—a version or alternative

vied—competed

Index

Check It Out!

Books

Block, Francesca Lia. 2004. *Weetzie Bat*. HarperTeen.

Poe, Edgar Allan. 2004. *The Essential Tales and Poems of Edgar Allan Poe*. Barnes & Noble Classics.

Rowell, Rainbow. 2013. *Fangirl: A Novel*. St. Martin's Griffin.

Videos

CNN. *Wingboarding: the next extreme sport in the sky.*

Guardian, The. *Extreme ironing: a champion returns.* https://www.theguardian.com/sport/video/2015/mar/19/extreme-ironing-phil-shaw-video.

No Man's Sky. http://www.no-mans-sky.com/about/.

Telegraph, The. *Bizarre World Bog Snorkelling Championship takes place in Wales.*

Websites

San Diego Comic Convention. *Comic-Con Front Page.* http://www.comic-con.org/cci.

The Bark. *Life with Dogs: At work, at home and on the go.* http://thebark.com/content/life-dogs.

Try It!

Imagine you are on the planning committee for the next Surprising Olympics. You are in charge of making an event brochure. Before you get to work, you've got some decisions to make:

- Make a list of strange (and fun) activities that can be included in the Surprising Olympics. Be sure to give each event a creative and unique name.

- Decide what you need for each event. What should the contestants bring with them? What tools will the planning committee provide?

- Select three events to highlight in the brochure. Use your power of persuasion to convince people to come watch or participate in the olympics.

- Fold a sheet of paper into three panels, and sketch each flap of the brochure. Make sure to highlight the main events on separate panels. Get creative, and include a quick illustration to go which each event.

- Complete the brochure by creating an engaging title page and back page. Include contact information for anyone who is interested in being a contestant, and list any additional things you want potential victors to know about the Surprising Olympics.

About the Author

Saskia Lacey is the author of *Jurassic Classics: The Prehistoric Masters of Literature* and *Technical Tales: How to Build a Plane*. Her potentially surprising hobbies include conversing with animals, cartoon binge watching, and spontaneous dancing.